Lingo Dingo
and the
Korean chef

Written by Mark Pallis
Illustrated by James Cottell

For my awesome sons - MP

For Leo and Juniper - JC

LINGO DINGO AND THE KOREAN CHEF

All rights reserved. This book or any portion thereof may not be reproduced or used in any manner whatsoever without the express written permission of the publisher except for the use of brief excerpts in a review.

Story edited by Natascha Biebow, Blue Elephant Storyshaping
First Printing, 2023
ISBN: 978-1-915337-51-1
NeuWestendPress.com

Lingo Dingo
and the
Korean chef

Written by Mark Pallis
Illustrated by James Cottell

**NEU WESTEND
— PRESS —**

This is Lingo. She's a Dingo and she loves helping.
Anyone. Anytime. Anyhow.

Lingo often helps her stylish neighbour Gunther, who lives by himself next door. She does a few jobs and has a nice chat. It makes Gunter feel good and it makes Lingo feel good too.

One day, Lingo arranged a special birthday party for Gunther. She even ordered a cake from a famous Korean chef.

There was a knock at the door, "It must be the cake!" said Lingo. But it was a monkey.

annyeong. naneun nono syepeulago hae
"안녕. 나는 노노 셰프라고 해.
geuleonde munjega saeng-gyeoss-eo
그런데 문제가 생겼어." he said.

Oh no. I can't speak Korean yet, thought Lingo. *Maybe '안녕' is like 'Hi'.*

안녕 = Hi; 나는 노노 셰프라고 해 = My name is Chef Nono;
그런데 문제가 생겼어 = But there is a problem.

"안녕," said Lingo. Chef Nono replied slowly,
mianhae. saeng-il keikeuleul mandeul su eobs-eo
"미안해. 생일 케이크르만들 수 없어."

"I don't understand," said Lingo. "But let me guess. You want..."

미안해 = sorry;
생일 케이크르만들 수 없어 = I cannot make the birthday cake

nae obeun-i gojang nass-eo,
"내 오븐이 고장 났어," explained Chef.
ni obeun-eul sayonghaedo doelkka?
"니 오븐을 사용해도 될까?"

Chef's oven must be broken thought Lingo. "I know! Let's bake the cake together," she said.

내 오븐이 고장 났어 = my oven is broken; 니 오븐을 사용해도 될까? = can I use your oven

Chef tapped his wrist. "몇시야? 아홉시야? 열시라고?" he asked.

myeochsiya?
ahobsiya? yeolsilago?

Lingo pointed at her watch.

"열한시! 지금 시작하자! 얼른!"

yeolhansi! jigeum sijaghaja! eolleun!

They only had one hour until the party.

몇시야? = what time is it?; 아홉시야? = is it nine o'clock; 열시라고 = ten o'clock; 열한시 = eleven o'clock; 지금 시작하자 = let's get started; 얼른 = hurry

Chef Nono and Lingo whizzed around the kitchen:

앞치마 두르고 = put on an apron; 거품기 = whisk
믹싱볼이 = mixing bowl

"버터, 설탕, 달걀 그리고 밀가루 좀 건내줄래,," said Chef.

beoteo, seoltang, dalgyal geuligo milgalu jom geonnaejullae

Lingo wasn't sure what those words meant, so she just grabbed fish, coffee and onions instead.

"생선, 커피, 그리고 양파. 맛 없어!" laughed Chef.

saengseon, keopi, geuligo yangpa. mas eobs-eo

건내줄래 = will you give me; 버터 = butter; 설탕 = sugar; 달걀 = eggs; 그리고 = and; 밀가루 = flour; 생선 = fish; 커피 = coffee; 그리고 양파 = onions; 맛 없어 = its tastes awful

Chef plopped butter, sugar, eggs and flour into a bowl. "So that's what 'beoteo, seoltang, dalgyal geuligo milgalu
버터, 설탕, 달걀 그리고 밀가루' means!" laughed Lingo.

naneun seokkgo, neoneun seokkgo, ulineun seokkneunda
"내가 섞고, 너도 섞고, 우리는 섞는다," said Chef and together they began to mix the cake.

내가 섞고 = I mix; 너도 섞고 = you mix; 우리는 섞는다 = we mix

"마지막으로 베이킹 파우더를 넣자. 두 숟갈," said Chef. Lingo guessed '베이킹 파우더를' meant baking powder, but how much?

Before she could ask, Chef hurried away, saying, "잠시만, 나 쉬 싸야해."

Lingo laughed, "I can guess what '나 쉬 싸야해' means!"

마지막으로 = finally; 넣자 = let's put; 베이킹 파우더를 = baking powder; 두 숟갈 = two spoonfulls; 잠시만 = hang on; 나 쉬 싸야해 = I need to do a wee wee

I wonder if this is too much? thought Lingo as she added ten spoonfulls of '베이킹 파우더를' to the mix.

She carefully put everything into the oven and before long, a sweet cakey smell filled the kitchen.

베이킹 파우더를 = baking powder

museun il-iya? eomcheong keo
"무슨 일이야? 엄청 커!" said Chef.

Lingo realised she had added too much baking powder.
"Sorry," she said sheepishly.

무슨 일이야? = whats the matter; 엄청 커 = it is so big

"I know what will make you feel better," said Lingo, kindly. 'Eat this '오이야'"

"맛없어. 나는 오이가 싫어" said Chef.

_{oiya}
_{mas-eobs-eo. naneun oiga silh-eo}

They were running out of time.

오이야 = cucumber; 맛없어 = it tastes awful; 나는 오이가 싫어 = I hate cucumbers

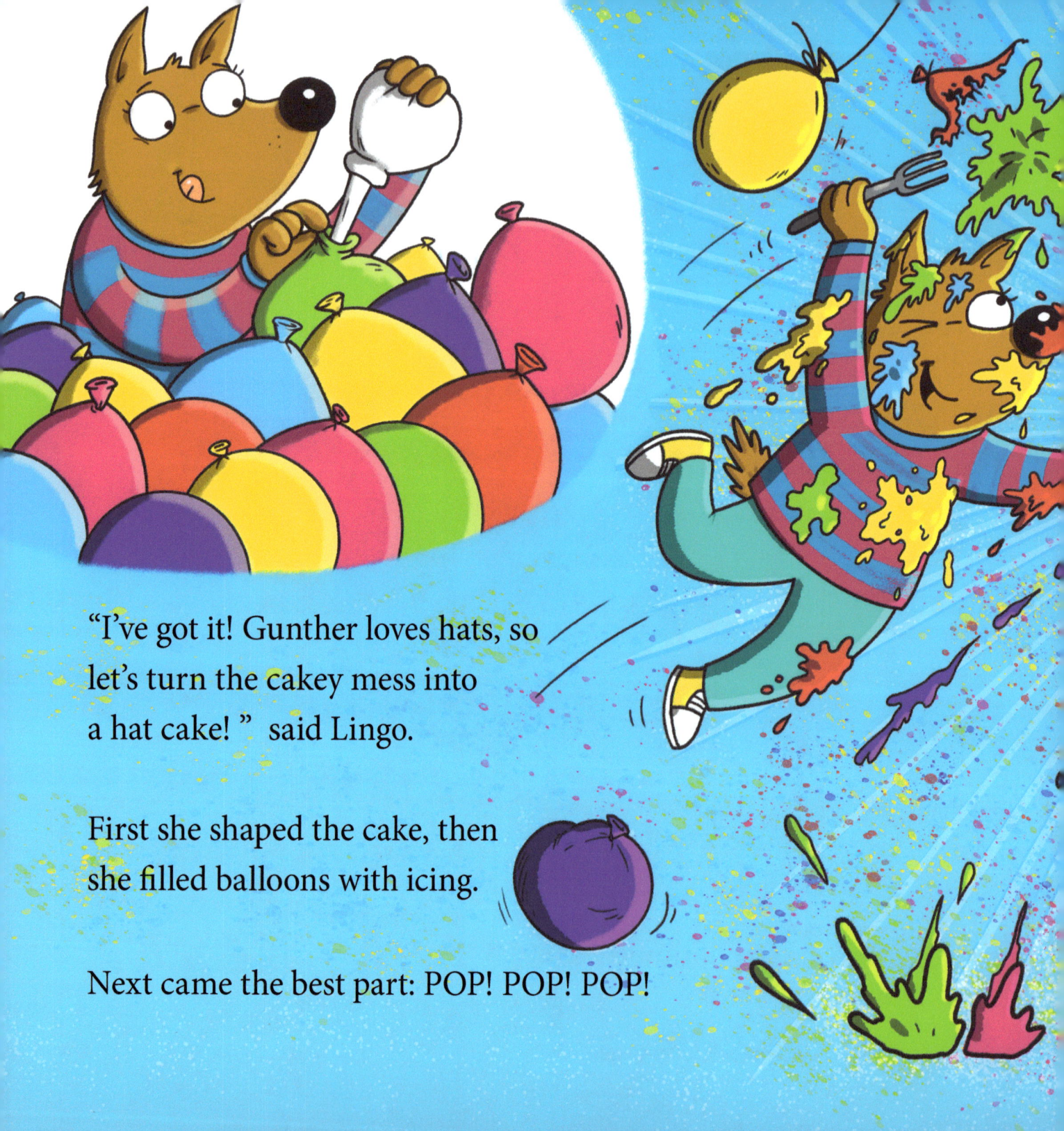

"I've got it! Gunther loves hats, so let's turn the cakey mess into a hat cake!" said Lingo.

First she shaped the cake, then she filled balloons with icing.

Next came the best part: POP! POP! POP!

It was a messy job but in the end, the cake looked fantastic.
ppalgangsaeg, olenjisaeg, nolangsaeg, chologsaeg, palansaeg. jeongmal ippeo
"빨강색, 오렌지색, 노랑색, 초록색, 파란색. 정말 이뻐!"said Chef.

빨강색 = red; 오렌지색 = orange; 노랑색 = yellow;
초록색 = green; 파란색 = blue; 정말 이뻐 = how pretty

There was a knock at the door.
"문!" said Chef.
It was Gunther, and he was wearing his special hat!

"Thank you. This makes me feel so special," said Gunther.
"You are special," replied Lingo.

문 = door

Gunter was thrilled with his cake.
Chef's deep voice sang "생일 축하 합니다 ..." _{saeng-il chugha habnida}

생일 축하 합니다..= Happy birthday

"불어봐!" said Chef.

bul-eobwa

Gunther blew out all the candles in one puff and everyone tucked in.

불어봐 = blow

nado meoggo, neodo meoggo, jeo namjado meoggo, jeo yeojado meoggo, jeo salamdeuldo meoggo
"나도 먹고, 너도 먹고, 저 남자도 먹고, 저 여자도 먹고, 저 사람들도 먹고," laughed Chef.

Oorineun meogneunda
"우리는 먹는다," added Lingo proudly.

나도 먹고 = I eat; 너도 먹고 = you eat; 저 남자도 먹고 = he eats;
저 여자도 먹고 = she eats; 저 사람들도 먹고 = they eat; 우리는 먹는다 = we eat

Baking a cake, helping a friend, learning a new language ... what a day!

But now it was time for bed. It was time to dream about all the fun things that might happen tomorrow.

Learning to love languages

An additional language opens a child's mind, broadens their horizons and enriches their emotional life. Research has shown that the time between a child's birth and their sixth or seventh birthday is a "golden period" when they are most receptive to new languages. This is because they have an in-built ability to distinguish the sounds they hear and make sense of them. The Story-powered Language Learning Method taps into these natural abilities.

How the story-powered language learning method works

We create an emotionally engaging and funny story for children and adults to enjoy together, just like any other picture book. Studies show that social interaction, like enjoying a book together, is critical in language learning.

Through the story, we introduce a relatable character who speaks only in the new language. This helps build empathy and a positive attitude towards people who speak different languages. These are both important aspects in laying the foundations for lasting language acquisition in a child's life.

As the story progresses, the child naturally works with the characters to discover the meanings of a wide range of fun new words. Strategic use of humour ensures that this subconscious learning is rewarded with laughter; the child feels good and the first seeds of a lifelong love of languages are sown.

For more information and free learning resources visit www.neuwestendpress.com

You can learn more words and phrases with these hilarious, heartwarming stories from **NEU WESTEND PRESS**

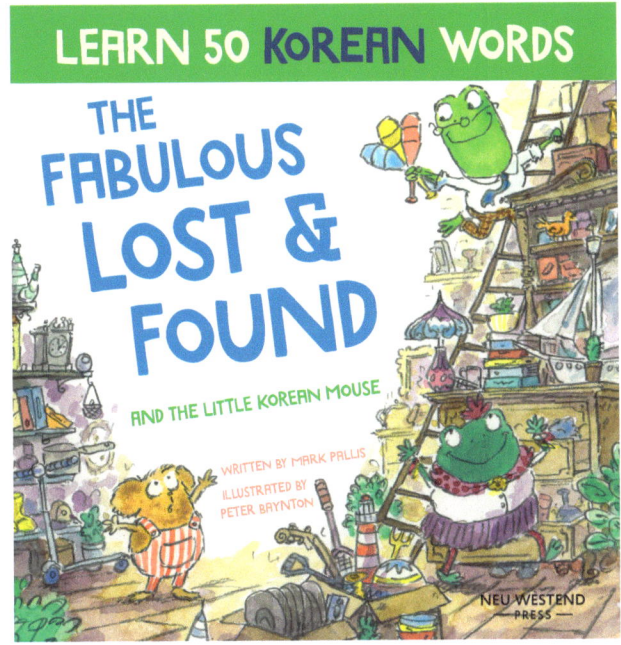

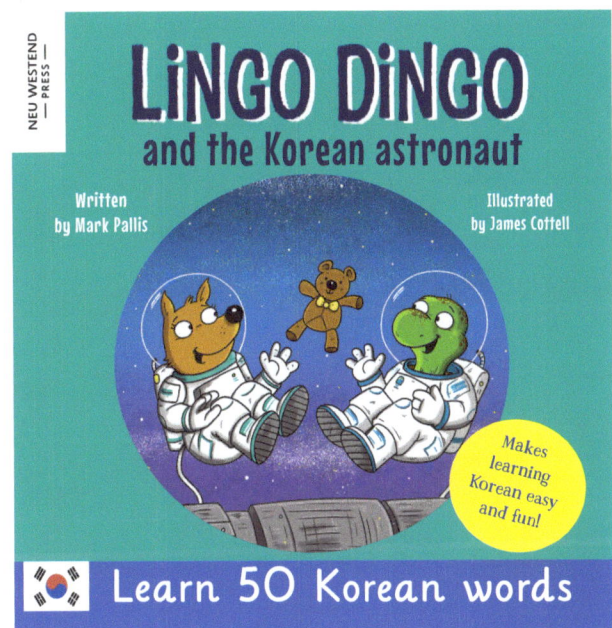

@MARK_PALLIS on twitter
www.markpallis.com

To download your FREE certifcate, and more cool stuff, visit
www.neuwestendpress.com

@jamescottell on INSTAGRAM
www.jamescottellstudios.co.uk

"I want people to be so busy laughing, they don't realise they're learning!"
Mark Pallis

Crab and Whale is the bestselling story of how a little Crab helps a big Whale. It's carefully designed to help even the most energetic children find a moment of calm and focus. It also includes a special mindful breathing exercise and affirmation for children.

Featured as one of Mindful.org's 'Seven Mindful Children's books'

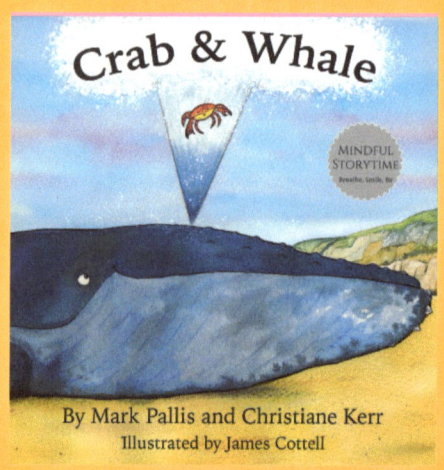

Do you call them hugs or cuddles?

In this funny, heartwarming rhyming story, you will laugh out loud as two loveable gibbons try to figure out if a hug is better than a cuddle and, in the process, learn how to get along.

A perfect story for anyone who loves a hug (or a cuddle!)

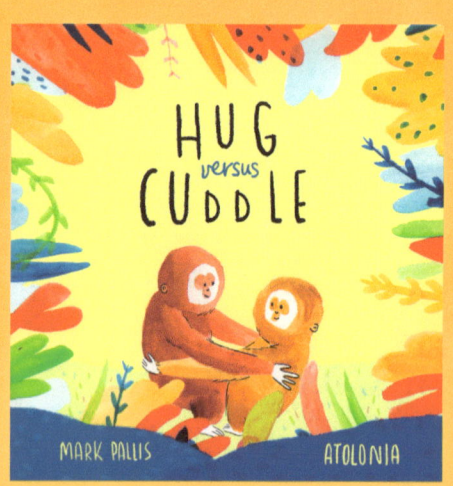

www.markpallis.com

www.ingramcontent.com/pod-product-compliance
Lightning Source LLC
Chambersburg PA
CBHW040021130526
44590CB00036B/44